ABC Reading eggs

My First Comprehension

By Sara Leman

Ages 5–7

Dear Parent or Carer,

This book is part of the **My First** series of **Reading Eggs** workbooks. **Reading Eggs** has proven to be very popular with parents, children and teachers. The **Reading Eggs** books and website have helped more than 20 million children worldwide learn to read.

Each vibrant book in the **My First** series includes a wide range of interesting activities that will help your child develop essential reading and writing skills. Written by experienced teachers and educators, the series supports what your child learns at school.

The pages are clear and uncluttered, with activities that build real skills. Activities are fun and motivate children to continue working and learning. Instructions are easy to follow and regular challenges entice children to extend their learning.

I hope that you and your child enjoy using this and other books in the series.

Kind regards, Katy Pike
Publisher

ABC Reading Eggs My First Comprehension

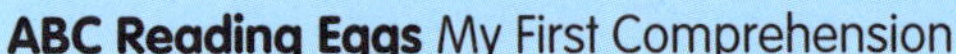

ISBN: 978-1-74215-165-6

Reprinted 2013, 2014, 2015, 2016, 2021, 2023

Distributed by:
Pascal Press
PO Box 250
Glebe NSW 2037

www.readingeggs.com
Written by Sara Leman
Publisher: Katy Pike
Editors: Sandra Iannella and Amanda Santamaria
Design and layout by Modern Art Production Group
Printed in China by 1010 Printing International Ltd

Contents

Comprehension activities to do at home

- Share a book with your child. Look at the picture on the front cover and ask what they think the story might be about. Point out the author and illustrator. Show them the back cover and read the blurb of the story.
- During reading, stop and ask your child what they think might happen next. Encourage them to tell you why they think events might happen and what effect they might have on the characters or the plot.
- After reading, discuss the story. Ask your child to retell stories or events and to offer their opinion. How did the story make them feel? What did they enjoy most? What did they dislike? Why?
- Encourage them to draw pictures of characters, scenes from the book or even design a new book cover for the story.
- Use hand puppets as a fun way to enhance reading time. Re-enact scenes from a favourite story and prompt your child to act out what the characters would do and say.
- Read stories by the same author and ask your child to think about the similarities and differences between the stories. This can also be done with a variety of books on the same topic and will encourage your child to begin drawing conclusions and building preferences.

- Provide your child with lots of different types of reading material. Let them look at magazines, brochures, leaflets, emails and lists that you have written. Point out the layout and purpose of the different pieces of writing.
- Sequencing skills are vital for comprehension development. Encourage your child to put things in order and follow directions. Read a simple comic strip together then cut it up and ask them to put it back in the correct order.
- Provide your child with a chart that illustrates the steps involved in brushing their teeth or making their bed. Work together on drawing the pictures and discuss each step in detail. Ask your child to recite the steps in order.
- Reading a recipe and following the instructions is an excellent way of building comprehension skills. Encourage your child to help you in the kitchen with cooking or baking. Read the recipe aloud and demonstrate how you have to follow each instruction to achieve a specific result.

Comprehension question types

Question type	Description	Example
• True or False? • Yes or No?	The answers to these questions can be found directly in the text. They can be answered by simply stating true or false, yes or no.	page 21
• Find the answers	The answers to these questions can be found directly in the text. In addition, some questions may require the child to draw upon their own knowledge.	page 41
• What's missing?	The child fills in the blanks with a suitable word.	page 34
• Finding out	The child is required to use information from the text in order to answer a number of questions.	page 56
• What happened?	These questions practise sequencing skills. The child is asked to put things in order. The tasks may be directly related to the story or based on the child's personal experience.	page 63
• The main idea	The child needs to determine the type of text and the central theme.	page 11

Question type	Description	Example
• Label it	The child labels a diagram based on knowledge they have acquired from reading the text.	page 54
• Step-by-step	These questions require the child to read and follow a series of instructions.	page 29
• Match-up	The child applies information from the text to a series of matching activities.	page 51
• Your turn • What do you think	These questions require a personal response to the text. They draw upon the child's own experiences.	page 69
• What happens next	The child provides an alternative ending to a story or predicts what they think will happen next.	page 25

Book 1 • Can you see?

Read the story

Can you see Sam?

Can you see the 3 bats?

Can you see the 4 bees?

Can you see the 5 cats?

I can see.

1 True or false? Colour the bats blue if they are true. Colour the bats red if they are false.

2 What happened? Number the events in the story in the correct order from 1 – 5.

Can you see the 5 cats?

I can see.

Can you see the 4 bees?

Can you see the 3 bats?

Can you see Sam?

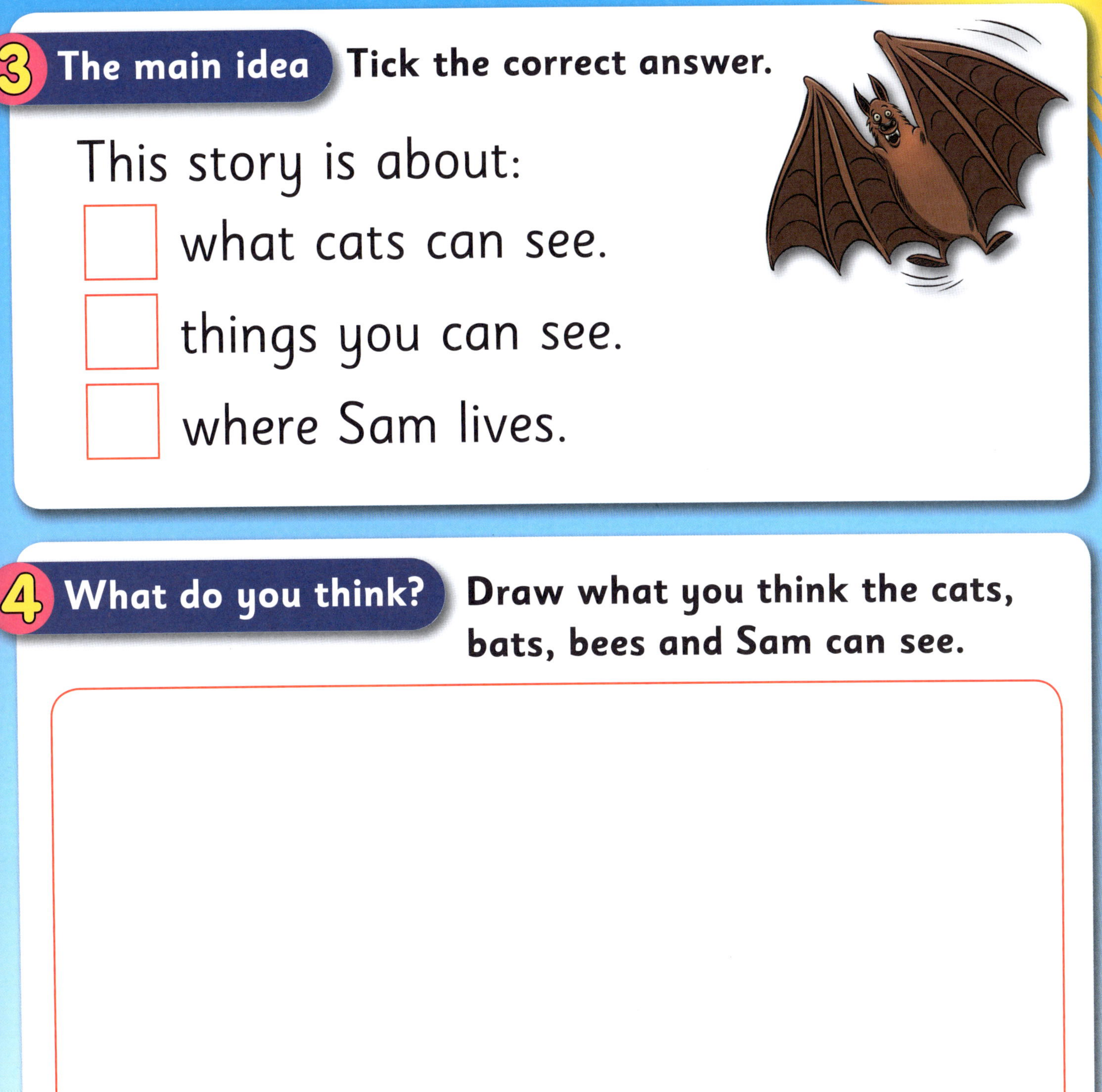

3 The main idea

Tick the correct answer.

This story is about:

- [ ] what cats can see.
- [ ] things you can see.
- [ ] where Sam lives.

4 What do you think?

Draw what you think the cats, bats, bees and Sam can see.

5 Match-up

Write the words under the correct picture. You can use some words more than once.

six legs eyes tail wings
four legs mouth purr

6 Your turn

Draw and write 4 things that you can see.

Book 2 • Dan

Read the story

I am Dan.
Dan has an ant in a hat.

He has a fat cat and a fat rat.
Dan has a man in a van.

He has Matt the bad ant.
He has a cat and a bat.

He has a map in a can.
Dan can see Zee the Bee.

1 Find the answers

Colour the correct answers.

Dan has
- a flat mat.
- a fat cat.

The man is
- in the van.
- on a can.

Matt is a
- bad ant.
- fat cat.

Dan's map is
- on the bat.
- in a can.

Dan can see
- a tree.
- Zee the Bee.

2 The main idea

Tick the correct answer.

This story is about:

- [ ] Dan at school.
- [ ] Zee the Bee.
- [ ] Dan and his toys.

3 Match up

Match each character to its object.

4 Step-by-step Follow each step to complete the map.

Draw:

- a fat cat under the tree.
- a hat on the cat.
- a rat on the can.
- a bee in the sea.

5 What happens next?

Write and draw what you think happens next.

Dan can see Zee the Bee.

6 Your turn

Dan has a lot of toys. What are your three favourite toys?

Book 3 • Cat and fish

Read the story

The fish has a tin.
The fish has a fin.

The cat can see the fish.
The cat sits and sits.

The fish can see the cat.
The fish hid in the tin.

The cat can see the fin.
Zap! The fish has a pin.
The cat ran.

1 Yes or no? Colour yes or no.

The fish is in the bin.

yes no

The cat sees the fish.

yes no

The cat wants to eat the fish.

yes no

The cat sees a dog.

yes no

2 What happened?

Number the pictures from the story in the correct order from 1 – 3.

☐ ☐ ☐

3 The main idea

Tick the correct answer.

This story is about:

☐ what fish like to eat.

☐ a bad cat and a clever fish.

☐ a sleepy cat.

4 What do you think?

What do you think the fish and the cat are saying? Write it in the bubbles.

5 Your turn **Draw a picture for each sentence.**

There is a pin in the fish's tin.

The fish zaps the cat with the pin.

The cat runs away.

6 What happens next?

Write and draw what you think happens next.

The cat ran.

Book 4 • The Big Queen

Read the story

The Queen has lots of big things. The Queen has a big ring. "I like my big ring," she said.

The Queen has a big crown. "I like my big crown," she said.

The Queen has a big dress. "I like my big dress," she said.

The Queen has a big castle. "Do you like my big castle?"

1 True or false?

Colour the crowns blue if they are true.
Colour the crowns red if they are false.

2 The main idea

Tick the correct answer.

This story is about:

- ☐ the Queen's new bed.
- ☐ a queen who likes big things.
- ☐ the Queen's big nose.

3 Match up

Match each person to their things.

4 Step-by-step

Follow each step to decorate the crown.

- Draw 5 diamonds ♦ on the crown.
- Colour the diamonds green.
- Draw 3 stars ★ on the crown.
- Colour the stars red.
- Colour the crown yellow.

5 Your turn

Put a ✓ next to the things that the Queen will like. Put a ✗ next to the things that she will not like.

6 What do you think?

The Queen has a big bed. Draw what you think her bedroom looks like.

Complete the sentence.

In her big castle, the Queen has a big ______________

____

Book 5 • Fox, rocks, socks and tops

Read the story

This is a fox. The fox got a box.

The fox got lots of boxes. Boxes! Boxes! What's in the boxes?

The fox got lots of rocks. The fox got lots of socks. The fox got a top in a box.

A top! A top! A fox on a top is a top fox.

1 True or false?

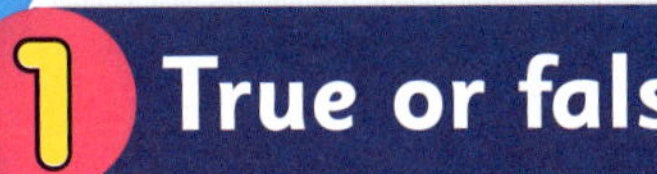

Colour the boxes blue if they are true.
Colour the boxes red if they are false.

The fox got:

a box	some socks	a pot
some spots	a cot	lots of rocks
	lots of boxes	a top

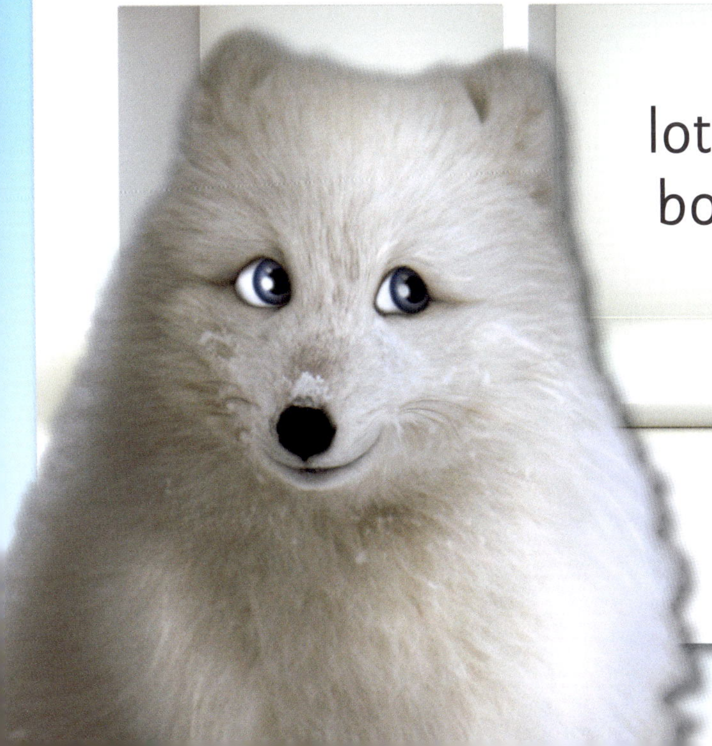

2 What's missing?

Use the pictures to help you complete the sentences.

lots box top fox

This is a

__________ .

The fox got a

__________ .

He got __________

of rocks.

This is a

__________ fox.

3 The main idea

Tick the correct answer.

This story is about:

- [ ] a lot of foxes.
- [ ] a fox with lots of boxes.
- [ ] a box full of foxes.

4 What do you think?

Who do you think the box of socks is from?

____

____

What do you think might be in one of the other boxes?

____

____

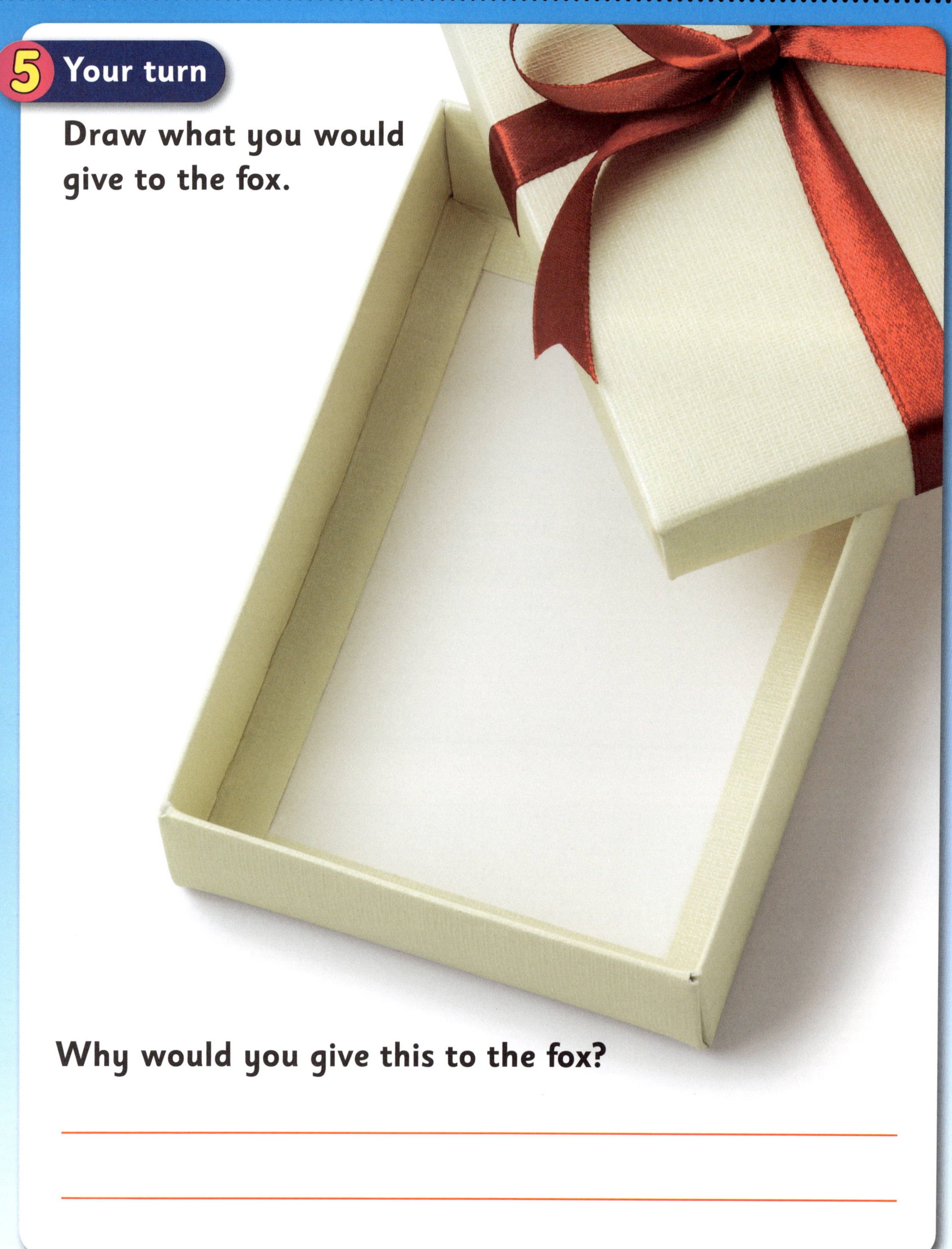

5 Your turn

Draw what you would give to the fox.

Why would you give this to the fox?

What happened?

Number the pictures in the correct order from 1 – 4.

Fun spot 1

1 **Complete the crossword.**

bee rabbits wings
stars woof grass

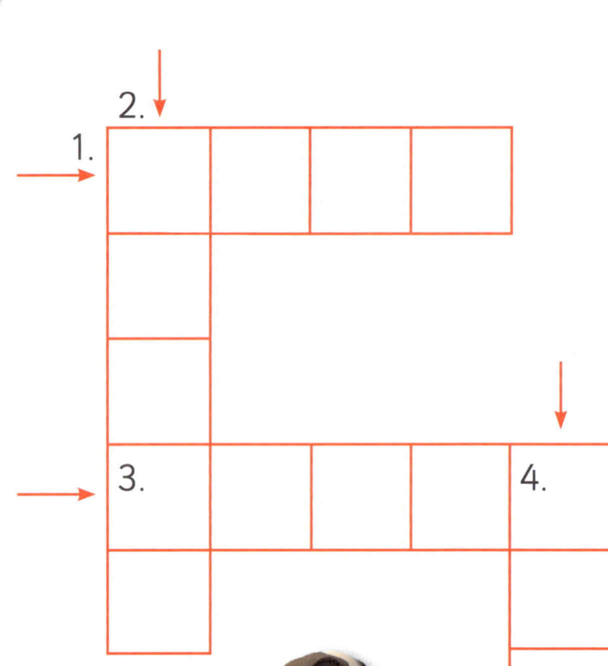

Clues

1 Dogs say "__________!"

2 Birds use __________ to fly.

3 Sheep eat lots of __________ .

4 __________ twinkle in the sky.

5 __________ love crunchy carrots.

6 "Buzzzzz," said the __________ .

What do you think they are saying?

Book 6 • Me

Read the story

I can kick. I can jump.
Look at me jump.

I can eat. I can climb.
Look at me climb.

I can draw. I can laugh.
Look at me laugh.

I can read. Look at me read.
I can sleep.

1 Find the answers

Answer the questions.

What can she do?

She can ______________________ .

What can she do?

She can ______________________ .

What can she do?

She can ______________________ .

What can she do?

____

2 The main idea

Tick the correct answer.

'Me' is:

☐ about real life.

☐ a story.

3 Match up

Match each word to a picture.

kick

climb

draw

read

sleep

eat

4 Step-by-step

Follow each step to fill up the lunchbox.

I can eat ...

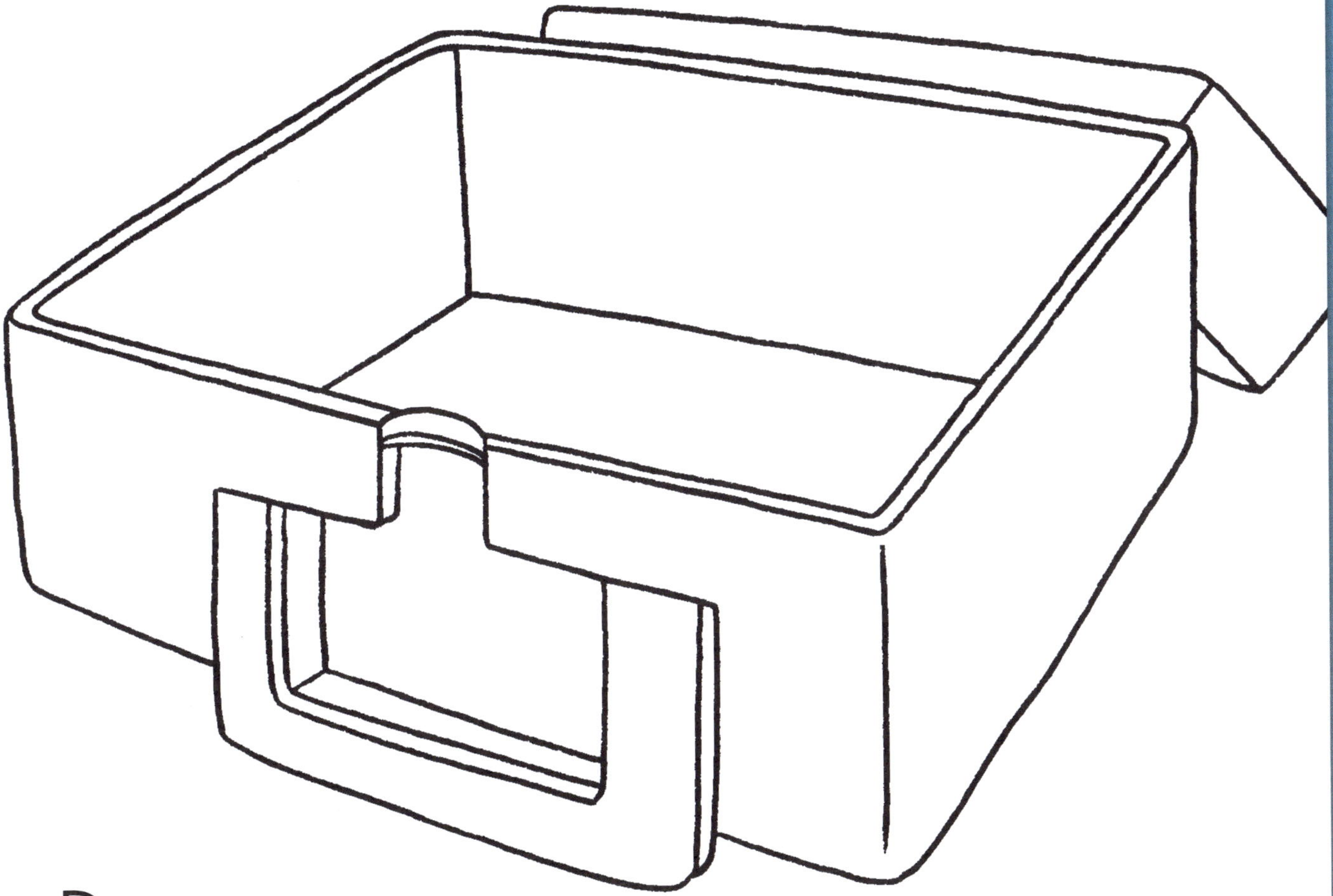

Draw:

- a sandwich.
- an apple.
- a banana.
- a tub of yoghurt.
- a bottle of water.

What can you do? Colour the face if you can do what it says.

I can swim.

I can sing

I can ride a bike.

I can fly.

I can hop.

I can skate.

I can draw.

I can smile.

I can count to ten.

6 What happened?

Number the steps in the correct order from 1 – 4.

I wash with soap. 

I dry my hands. 

I wet my hands. 

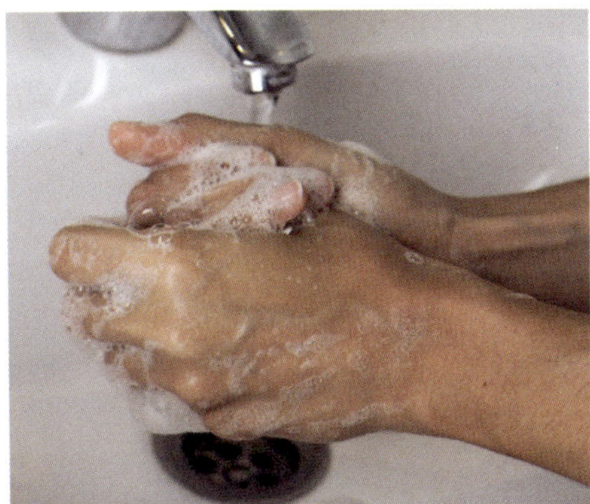

I rinse my hands. ☐

Book 7 • Fluff the duck

Read the story

Can Fluffy Duck drive a truck?
No! Fluffy Duck gets stuck in the muck.

Is Fluffy Duck out of luck?
Tom the Dog can see the bog.

Tom the Dog gets lots of logs.
Fluffy Duck can drive her truck.

"I am in luck," said Fluffy.
"I can drive my truck!"

1 Yes or no? Colour yes or no.

Fluffy is a hen.

yes no

Fluffy gets stuck in some muck.

yes no

Fluffy is feeling very lucky.

yes no

Tom the Dog helps Fluffy.

yes no

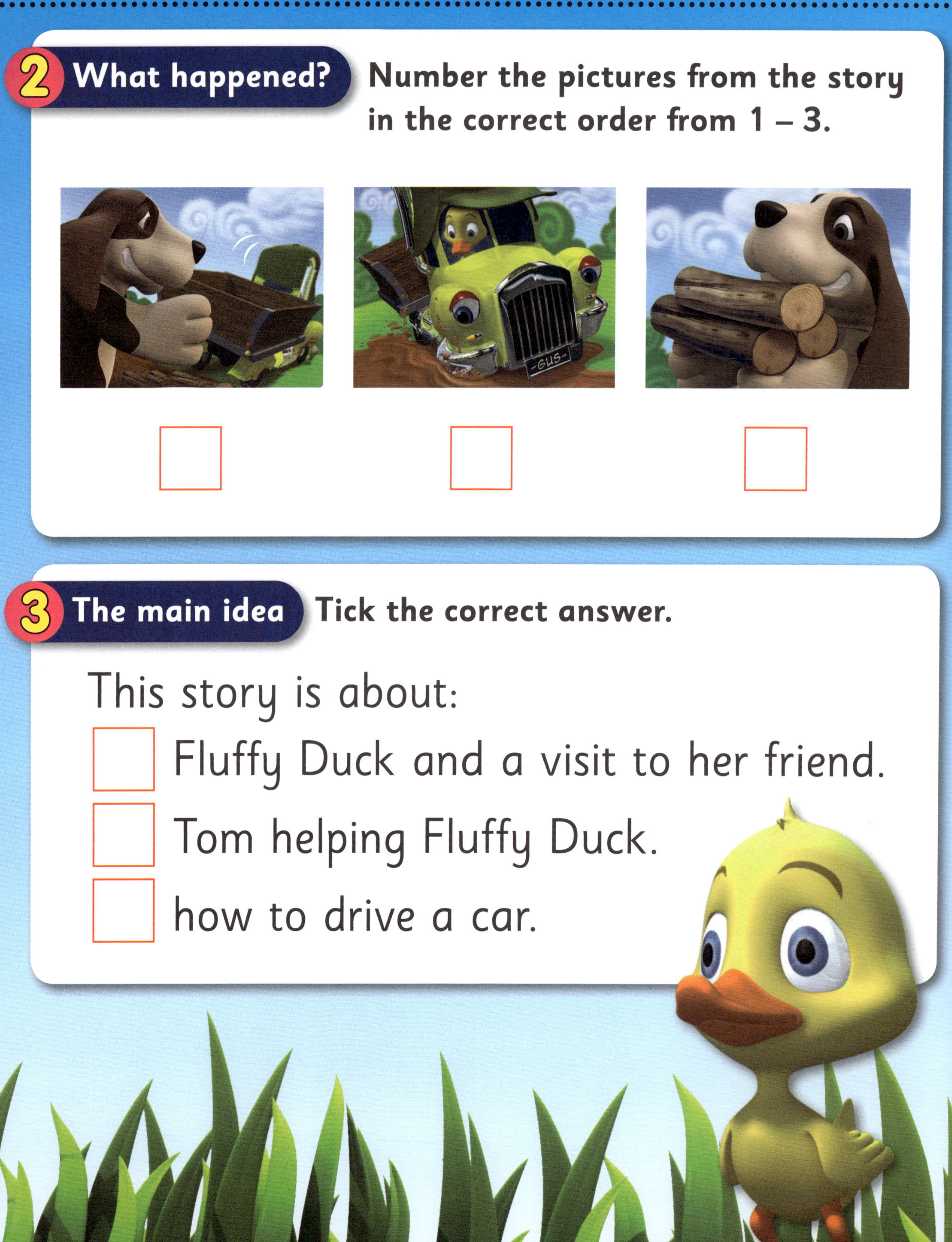

2 What happened?

Number the pictures from the story in the correct order from 1 – 3.

☐ ☐ ☐

3 The main idea

Tick the correct answer.

This story is about:

☐ Fluffy Duck and a visit to her friend.

☐ Tom helping Fluffy Duck.

☐ how to drive a car.

4 What happens next?

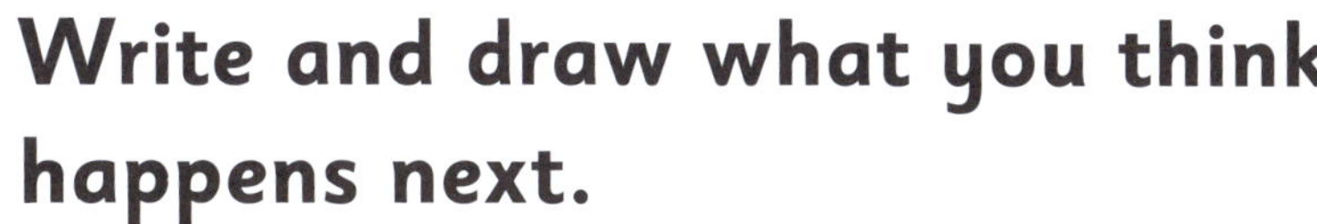

Write and draw what you think happens next.

"I can drive my truck!"

5 What do you think?

What do you think Fluffy Duck is thinking? Write it in the bubble.

What do you think Fluffy Duck would say to Tom at the end of the story?

6 Match-up

Everyone is stuck! Draw lines to show what everyone needs.

Book 8 • Dogs and cats

Read the information

This is a dog and a cat.

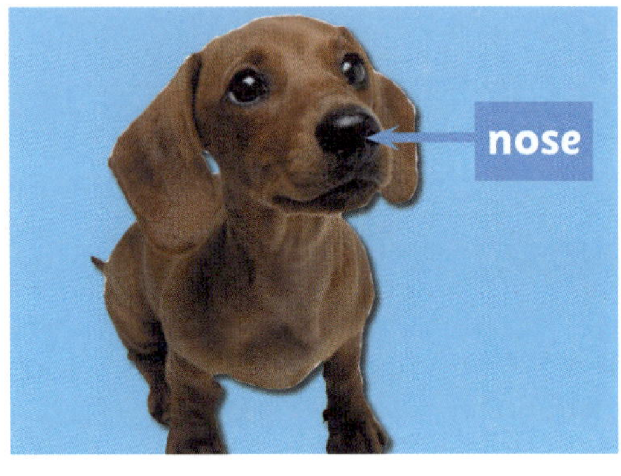

Dogs have one nose.
Cats have one nose.

Dogs have two eyes.
Cats have two eyes.

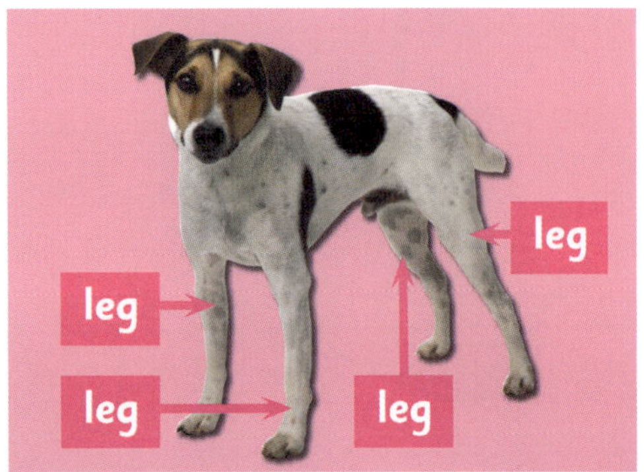

Dogs have four legs.
Cats have four legs.

1 **True or false?** Colour the animal blue if it is true. Colour the animal red if it is false.

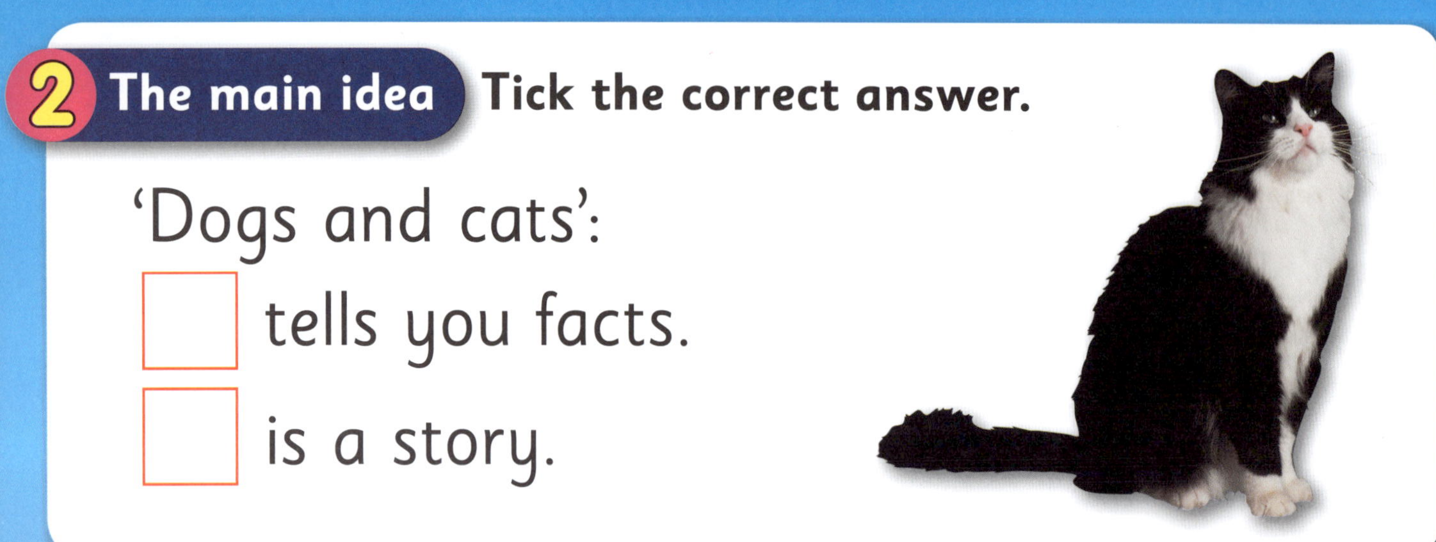

2 The main idea

Tick the correct answer.

'Dogs and cats':

- [ ] tells you facts.
- [ ] is a story.

3 Label it

Use the words to label the picture.

- eye
- nose
- leg

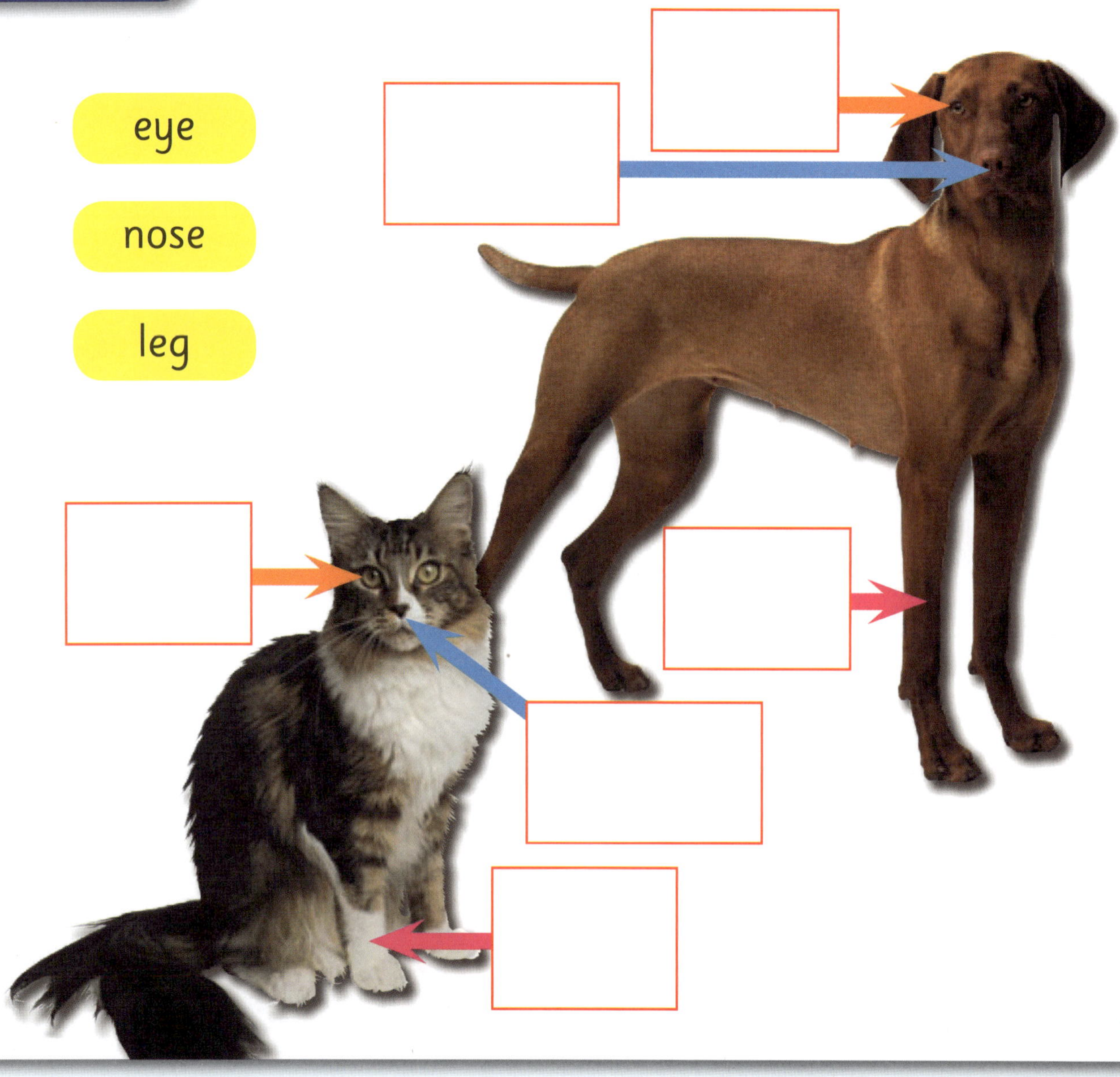

4 Find the answers

What things do cats and dogs have that are the same?

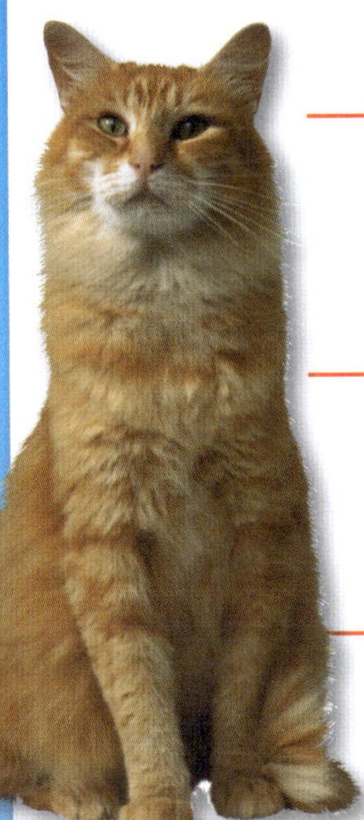

What things do cats and dogs have that are **not** the same?

cats	dogs

This is a fact book about dogs.

Contents **page**

Answer these questions.

What is this book about?

____

How many chapters are there?

____

What will page 5 tell you?

____

What is chapter 1 called?

____

Draw a picture of a cat or dog.
Answer the questions about your picture.

What is it called?

____

What does it eat?

____

What does it do?

____

Book 9 • My five senses

Read the information

We have five senses.
I can see with my eyes.
I can see a butterfly.

I can hear with my ears.
I can hear music.

I can smell with my nose.
I can smell a flower.

I can taste with my tongue.
I can taste an apple.

I can touch with my hands.
I can touch the sand.

Colour yes or no.

We have three senses.

yes no

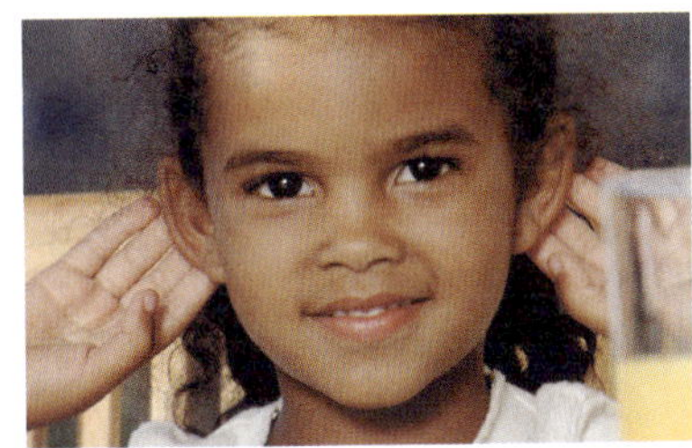

I can hear with my ears.

yes no

I can touch things with my hands.

yes no

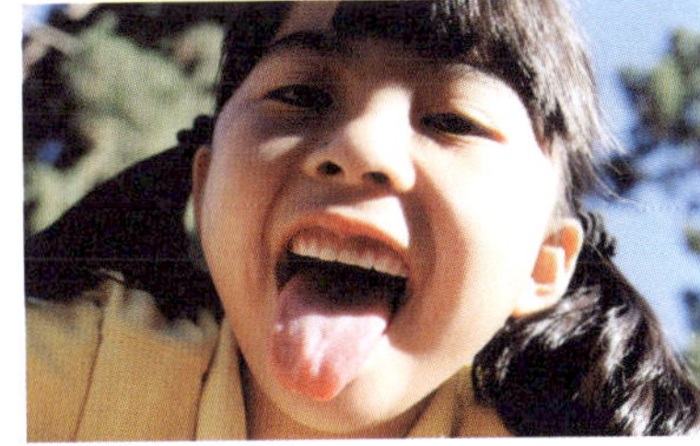

My tongue helps me to see.

yes no

2 The main idea

Tick the correct answer.

'My five senses' is:

☐ a story.

☐ about real life.

3 Match up

Complete the list of senses.
Match them to the correct body part.

s ee

t __________

t __________

h __________

s __________

4 Find the answers

What things can humans and cats do that are the same?

What things can humans and cats do that are **not** the same?

humans	cats

5 Your turn Write three things that you can ...

6 What happened?

Number the events in order from 1 – 4. Write what happens next.

Chop the apple. 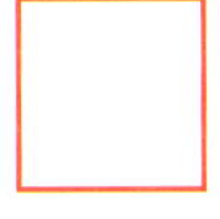

Get an apple. 

Put the apple on a plate. 

Peel the apple. ☐

Then ______________________________

Book 10 • Meg's birthday

Read the story

Meg the Hen is seven.
Today is her birthday party.

Meg has seven hats and seven cups. She has seven plates and seven bags.

Sam, Jazz, Sid, Fluff, Tom and Flobby get a hat, a cup, a plate and a bag.

Meg gets a hat, a cup, a plate and a bag.
Happy birthday to you, Meg!

1 Find the answers

Look back at the story. Write the answers.

Whose birthday is it?

How old is she?

How many bags does she have?

Who came to the party?

2 The main idea

Tick the correct answer.

This story is about:

- [ ] Flobby's birthday party.
- [ ] Meg's birthday presents.
- [ ] Meg's 7th birthday party.

3 Match up

Match each word to the correct picture.

hats		cake
shells	birthday	sea
cups		plates
tail	mermaid	fish

birthday

mermaid

4 Step-by-step

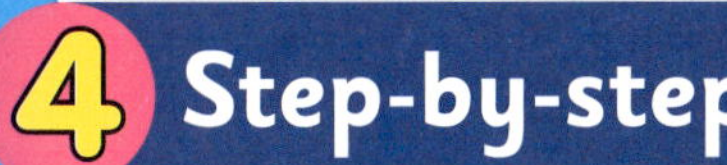

Follow each step to decorate the cake.

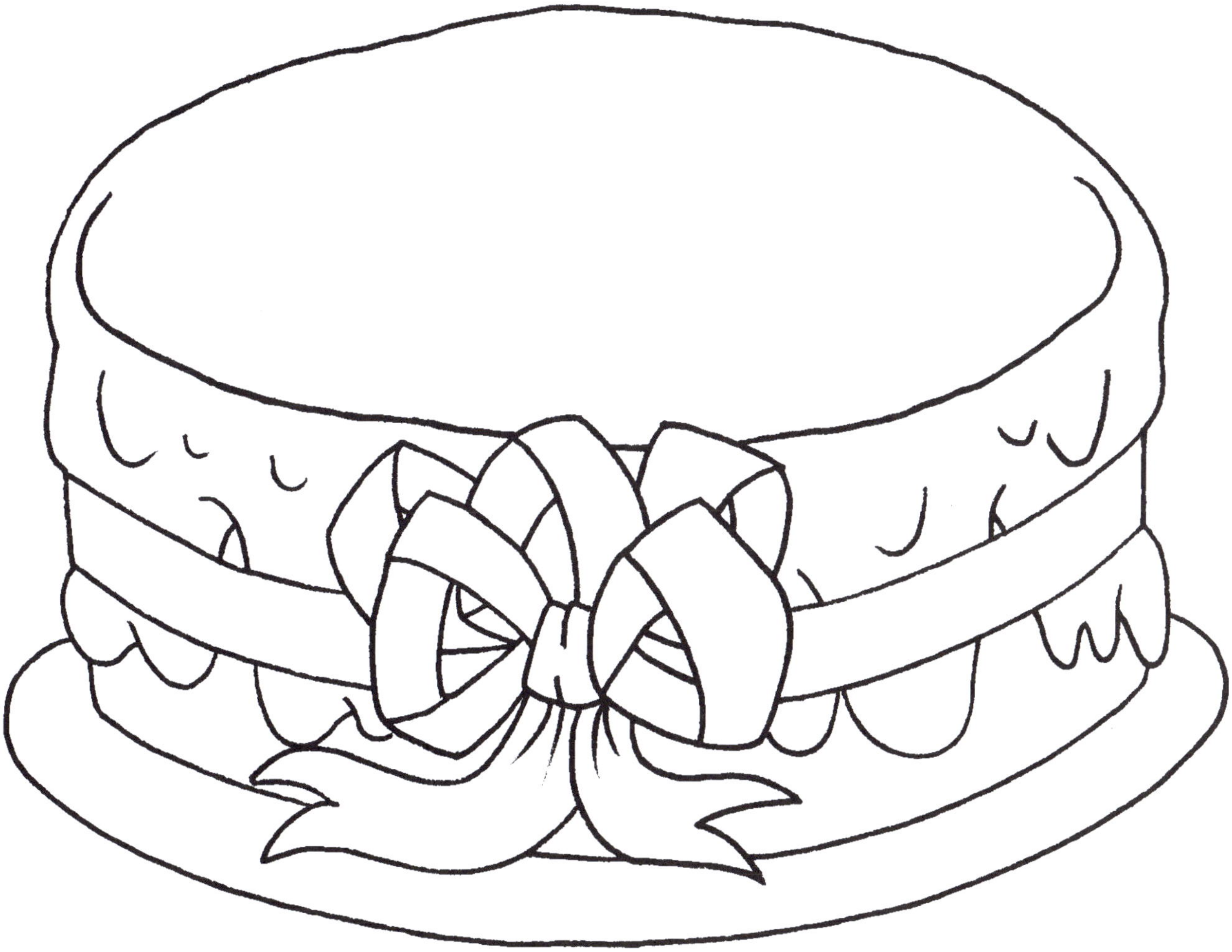

- Write **Meg** on the cake.
- Draw seven candles on the cake.
- Draw seven spotty eggs on the cake.
- Colour the bow purple.
- Colour the cake pink.

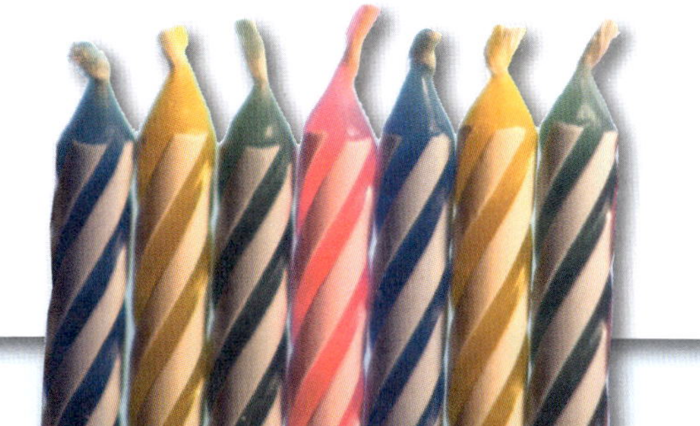

5 What happened?

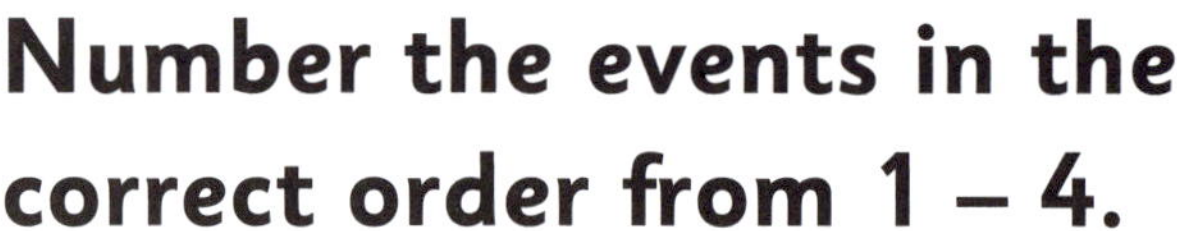

Number the events in the correct order from 1 – 4.

Put it in the oven. ☐

Put everything into a bowl. ☐

Here is the birthday cake! ☐

Mix it all up well. ☐

Your turn

Complete the party invitation.

PARTY!

(Your name) ______________________

is having a birthday party.

Day: ______________________

Place: ______________________

____

Time: ______________________

You will need to wear:

____

Fun spot 2

1 **Make up a cover for this new book:**

Title: Frog's birthday party

Written by: Lily Pond

Remember
You will also need to draw a picture on the front cover.

2 **Read how to find the buried treasure. Draw the way on the map.**

- Start at the ship. Swim to the rocks.
- Walk to the tree.
- Walk to the hill.
- Climb up to the top of the hill.
- Walk down the hill.
- Walk to the cave. Dig here for treasure!

Answers • Pages 8 to 23

Book 1 • Can you see?
Read the story
Can you see Sam?
Can you see the 3 bats?
Can you see the 4 bees?
Can you see the 5 cats?
I can see.
8
Can you see?
1 True or false? Colour the bats blue if they are true. Colour the bats red if they are false.
There are 5 bats.
There are 4 bees.
You can see Sam.
You can see rats.
There are 5 cats.
9

2 What happened? Number the events in the story in the correct order from 1 – 5.
Can you see the 5 cats? 4
I can see. 5
Can you see the 4 bees? 3
Can you see the 3 bats? 2
Can you see Sam? 1
10
Can you see?
3 The main idea Tick the correct answer.
This story is about:
☐ what cats can see.
☑ things you can see.
☐ where Sam lives.
4 What do you think? Draw what you think the cats, bats, bees and Sam can see.
Parent check
11

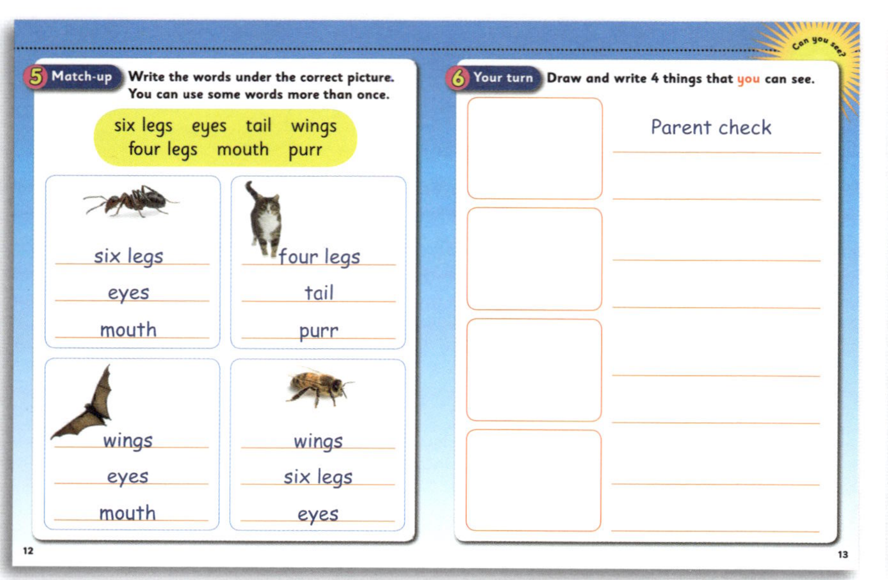
5 Match-up Write the words under the correct picture. You can use some words more than once.
six legs eyes tail wings four legs mouth purr
six legs
eyes
mouth
four legs
tail
purr
wings
eyes
mouth
wings
six legs
eyes
12
Can you see?
6 Your turn Draw and write 4 things that you can see.
Parent check
13

Book 2 • Dan
Read the story
I am Dan.
Dan has an ant in a hat.
He has a fat cat and a fat rat.
Dan has a man in a van.
He has Matt the bad ant.
He has a cat and a bat.
He has a map in a can.
Dan can see Zee the Bee.
14
Dan
1 Find the answers Colour the correct answers.
Dan has a flat mat. / a fat cat.
The man is in the van. / on a can.
Matt is a bad ant. / fat cat.
Dan's map is on the bat. / in a can.
Dan can see a tree. / Zee the Bee.
15

Dan

2 The main idea
Tick the correct answer.

This story is about:
- [ ] Dan at school.
- [ ] Zee the Bee.
- [x] Dan and his toys.

3 Match up
Match each character to its object.

4 Step-by-step
Follow each step to complete the map.

Parent check

Draw:
- a fat cat under the tree.
- a hat on the cat.
- a rat on the can.
- a bee in the sea.

5 What happens next?
Write and draw what you think happens next.

Dan can see Zee the Bee.

Parent check

6 Your turn
Dan has a lot of toys. What are your three favourite toys?

Parent check

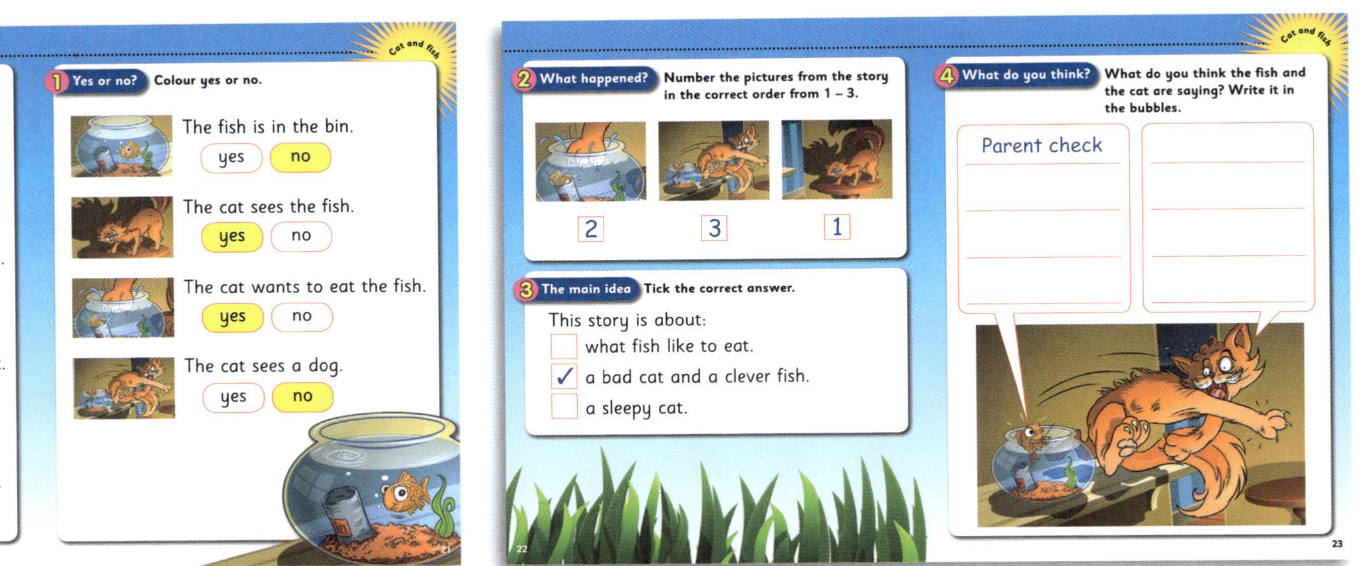

Book 3 • Cat and fish

Read the story

The fish has a tin.
The fish has a fin.

The cat can see the fish.
The cat sits and sits.

The fish can see the cat.
The fish hid in the tin.

The cat can see the fin.
Zap! The fish has a pin.
The cat ran.

Cat and fish

1 Yes or no?
Colour yes or no.

The fish is in the bin. yes **no**

The cat sees the fish. **yes** no

The cat wants to eat the fish. **yes** no

The cat sees a dog. yes **no**

2 What happened?
Number the pictures from the story in the correct order from 1 – 3.

2 3 1

3 The main idea
Tick the correct answer.

This story is about:
- [ ] what fish like to eat.
- [x] a bad cat and a clever fish.
- [ ] a sleepy cat.

Cat and fish

4 What do you think?
What do you think the fish and the cat are saying? Write it in the bubbles.

Parent check

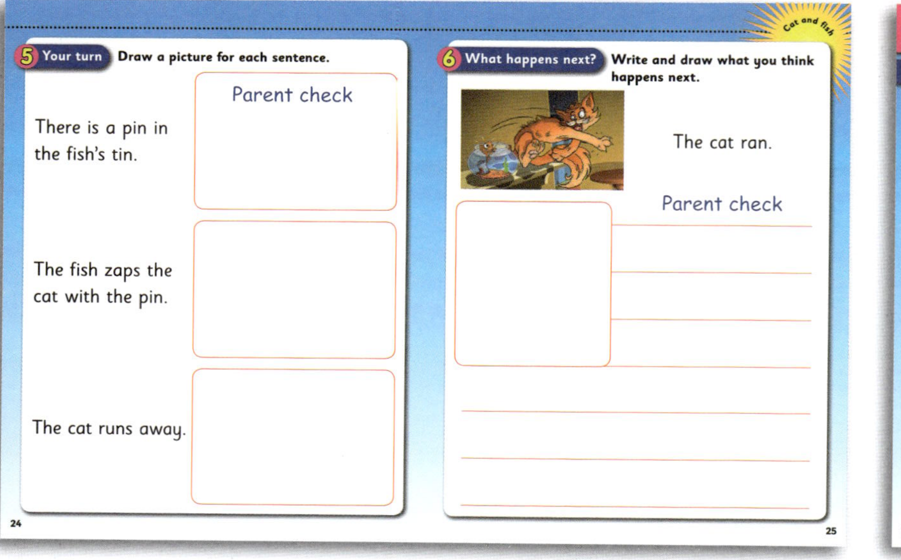
Cat and fish

5 Your turn Draw a picture for each sentence.

There is a pin in the fish's tin. — Parent check

The fish zaps the cat with the pin.

The cat runs away.

6 What happens next? Write and draw what you think happens next.

The cat ran.

Parent check

24 25

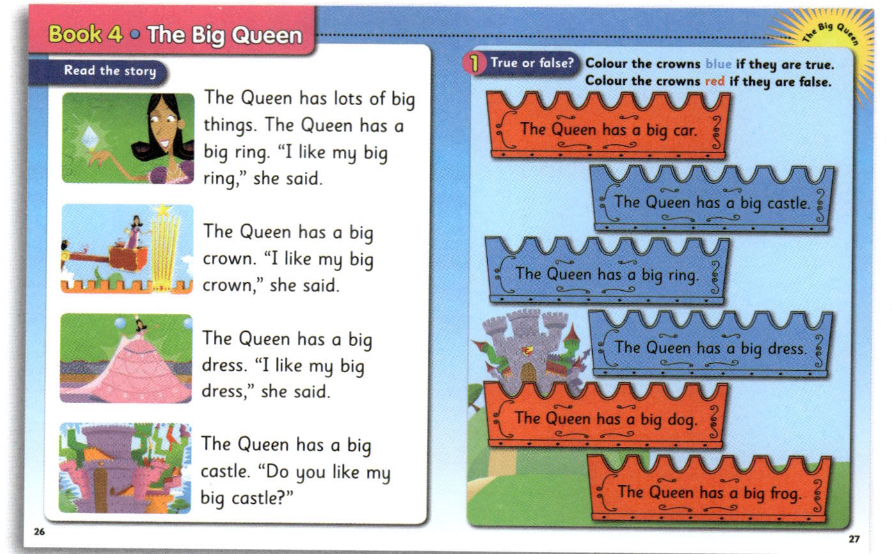
Book 4 • The Big Queen

Read the story

The Queen has lots of big things. The Queen has a big ring. "I like my big ring," she said.

The Queen has a big crown. "I like my big crown," she said.

The Queen has a big dress. "I like my big dress," she said.

The Queen has a big castle. "Do you like my big castle?"

The Big Queen

1 True or false? Colour the crowns blue if they are true. Colour the crowns red if they are false.

The Queen has a big car.

The Queen has a big castle.

The Queen has a big ring.

The Queen has a big dress.

The Queen has a big dog.

The Queen has a big frog.

26 27

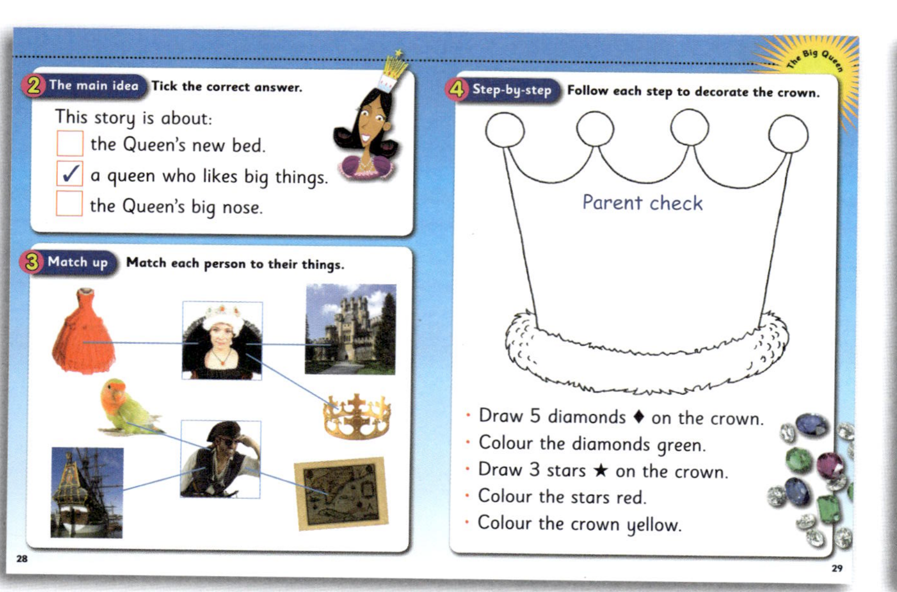
The Big Queen

2 The main idea Tick the correct answer.

This story is about:

- [ ] the Queen's new bed.
- [x] a queen who likes big things.
- [ ] the Queen's big nose.

3 Match up Match each person to their things.

4 Step-by-step Follow each step to decorate the crown.

Parent check

- Draw 5 diamonds ◆ on the crown.
- Colour the diamonds green.
- Draw 3 stars ★ on the crown.
- Colour the stars red.
- Colour the crown yellow.

28 29

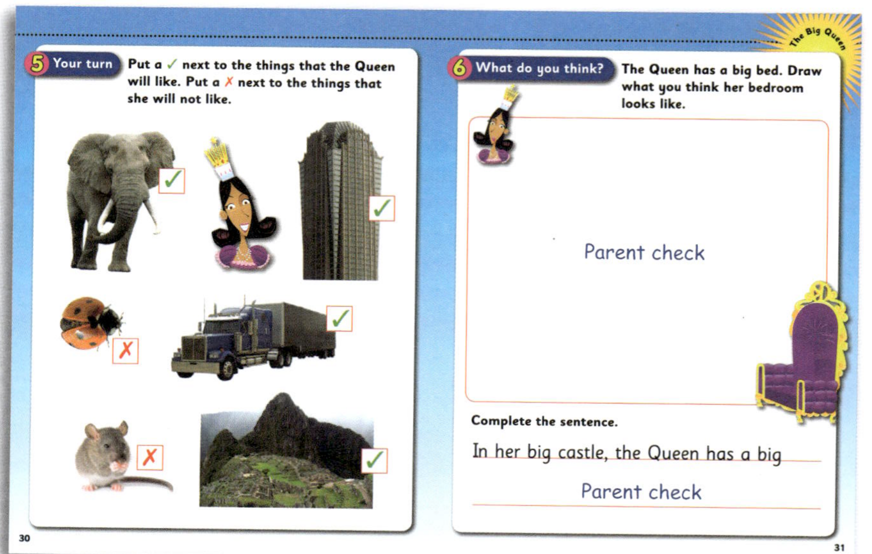
The Big Queen

5 Your turn Put a ✓ next to the things that the Queen will like. Put a ✗ next to the things that she will not like.

6 What do you think? The Queen has a big bed. Draw what you think her bedroom looks like.

Parent check

Complete the sentence.

In her big castle, the Queen has a big

Parent check

30 31

Book 5 • Fox, rocks, socks and tops

Read the story

This is a fox. The fox got a box.

The fox got lots of boxes. Boxes! Boxes! What's in the boxes?

The fox got lots of rocks. The fox got lots of socks. The fox got a top in a box.

A top! A top! A fox on a top is a top fox.

32

1 True or false? Colour the boxes blue if they are true. Colour the boxes red if they are false.

The fox got:

a box	some socks	a pot
some spots	a cot	lots of rocks
	lots of boxes	a top

33

2 What's missing? Use the pictures to help you complete the sentences.

lots box top fox

This is a fox.

The fox got a box.

He got lots of rocks.

This is a top fox.

34

3 The main idea Tick the correct answer.

This story is about:

- [ ] a lot of foxes.
- [x] a fox with lots of boxes.
- [ ] a box full of foxes.

4 What do you think? Who do you think the box of socks is from?

Parent check

What do you think might be in one of the other boxes?

Parent check

35

5 Your turn Draw what you would give to the fox.

Parent check

Why would you give this to the fox?

36

6 What happened? Number the pictures in the correct order from 1 – 4.

3 4 1 2

37

Fun spot 1

1 Complete the crossword.

bee rabbits wings stars woof grass

Clues

1 Dogs say " woof !"
2 Birds use wings to fly.
3 Sheep eat lots of grass .
4 Stars twinkle in the sky.
5 Rabbits love crunchy carrots.
6 "Buzzzzz," said the bee .

38

2 What do you think they are saying?

Parent check

Parent check

39

Answers • Pages 40 to 55

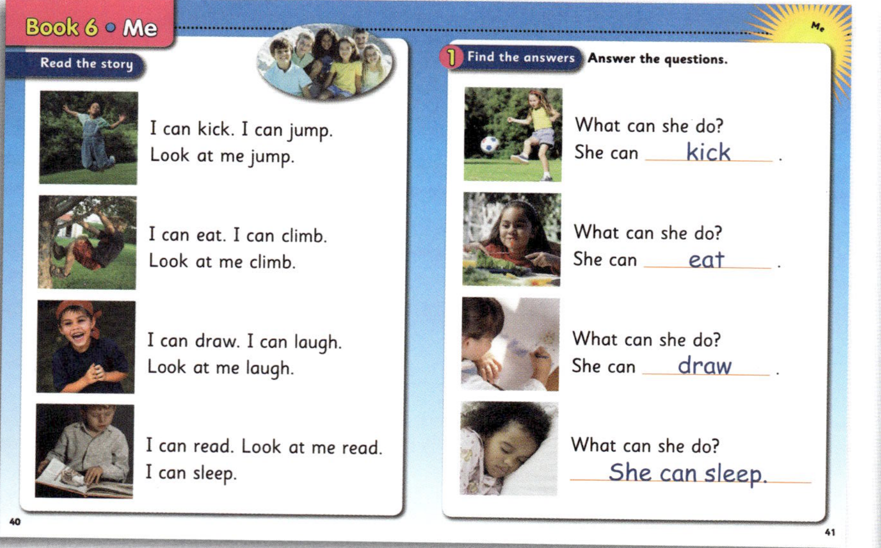

Book 6 • Me

Read the story

I can kick. I can jump.
Look at me jump.

I can eat. I can climb.
Look at me climb.

I can draw. I can laugh.
Look at me laugh.

I can read. Look at me read.
I can sleep.

40

1 Find the answers Answer the questions.

What can she do?
She can kick.

What can she do?
She can eat.

What can she do?
She can draw.

What can she do?
She can sleep.

41

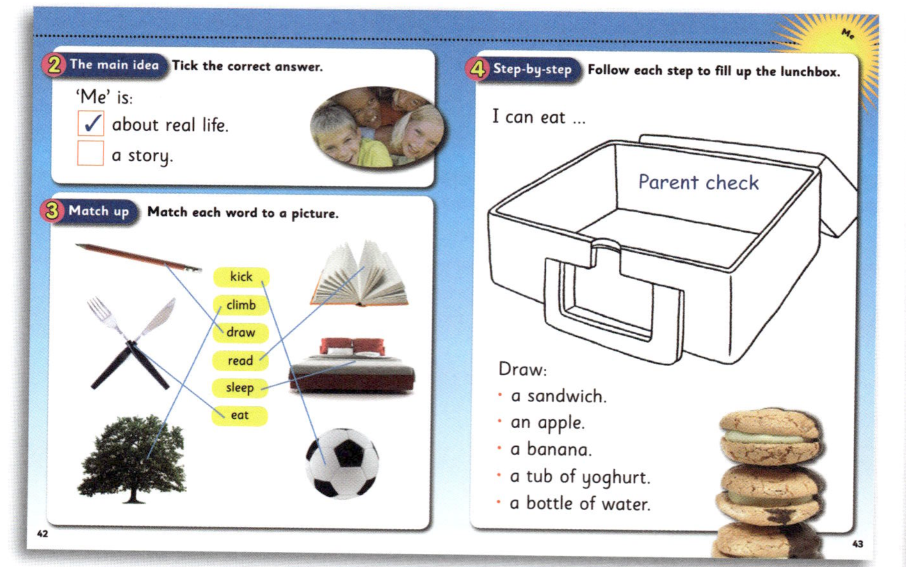

2 The main idea Tick the correct answer.

'Me' is:

- [x] about real life.
- [ ] a story.

3 Match up Match each word to a picture.

kick, climb, draw, read, sleep, eat

42

4 Step-by-step Follow each step to fill up the lunchbox.

I can eat ...

Parent check

Draw:

- a sandwich.
- an apple.
- a banana.
- a tub of yoghurt.
- a bottle of water.

43

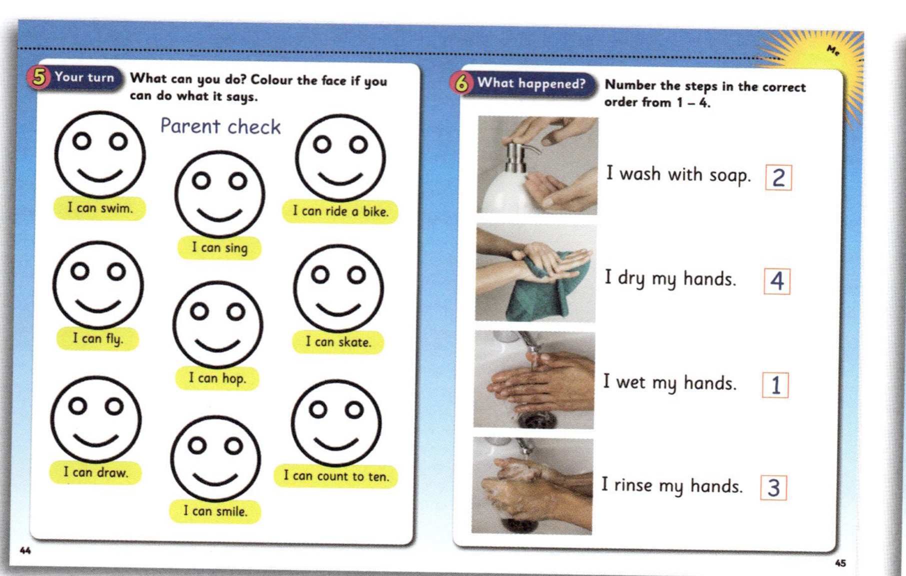

5 Your turn What can you do? Colour the face if you can do what it says.

Parent check

I can swim.
I can sing
I can ride a bike.
I can fly.
I can hop.
I can skate.
I can draw.
I can smile.
I can count to ten.

44

6 What happened? Number the steps in the correct order from 1 – 4.

I wash with soap.	2
I dry my hands.	4
I wet my hands.	1
I rinse my hands.	3

45

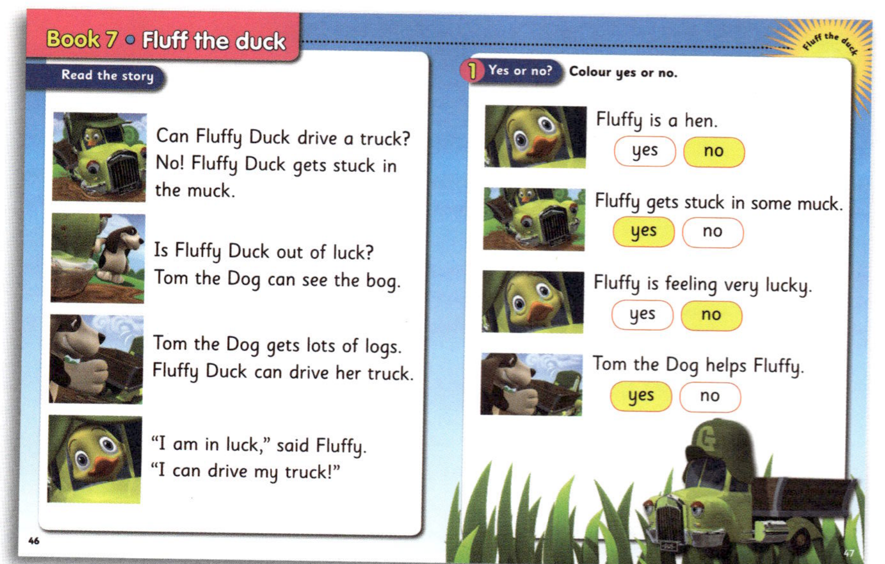

Book 7 • Fluff the duck

Read the story

Can Fluffy Duck drive a truck?
No! Fluffy Duck gets stuck in the muck.

Is Fluffy Duck out of luck?
Tom the Dog can see the bog.

Tom the Dog gets lots of logs.
Fluffy Duck can drive her truck.

"I am in luck," said Fluffy.
"I can drive my truck!"

46

1 Yes or no? Colour yes or no.

Fluffy is a hen.	no
Fluffy gets stuck in some muck.	yes
Fluffy is feeling very lucky.	no
Tom the Dog helps Fluffy.	yes

47

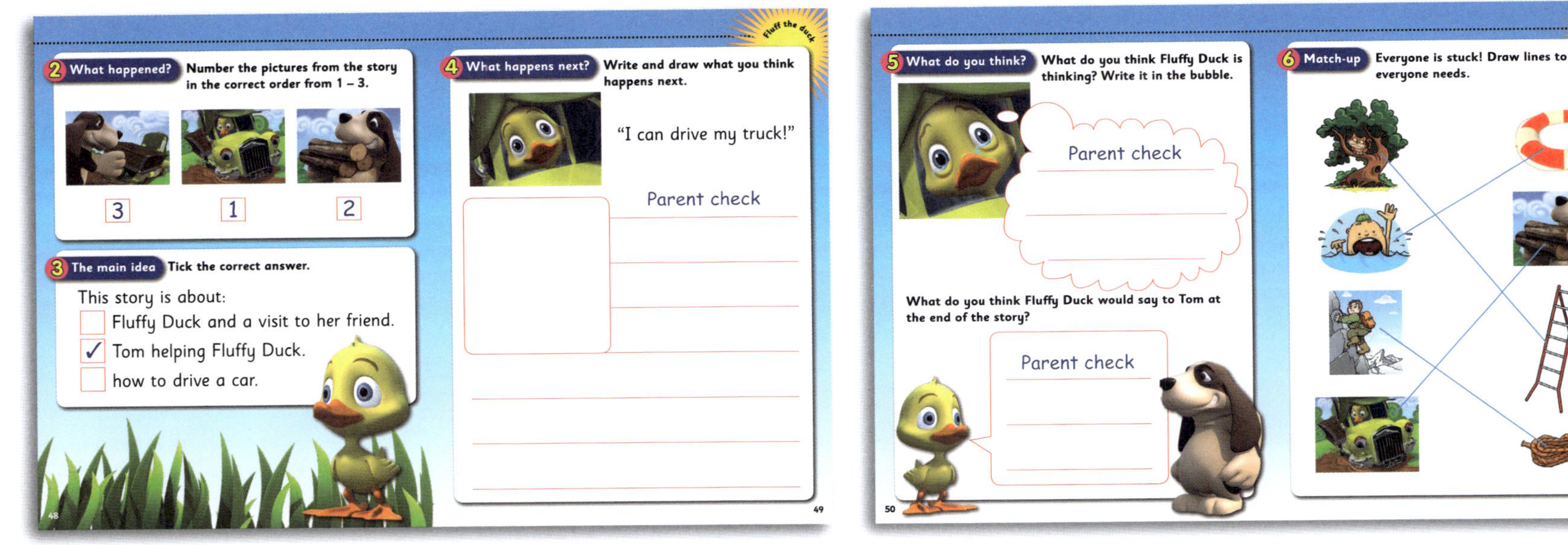

Fluff the duck

2 What happened? Number the pictures from the story in the correct order from 1 – 3.

3 1 2

3 The main idea Tick the correct answer.

This story is about:

- [ ] Fluffy Duck and a visit to her friend.
- [x] Tom helping Fluffy Duck.
- [ ] how to drive a car.

48

4 What happens next? Write and draw what you think happens next.

"I can drive my truck!"

Parent check

49

5 What do you think? What do you think Fluffy Duck is thinking? Write it in the bubble.

Parent check

What do you think Fluffy Duck would say to Tom at the end of the story?

Parent check

50

6 Match-up Everyone is stuck! Draw lines to show what everyone needs.

51

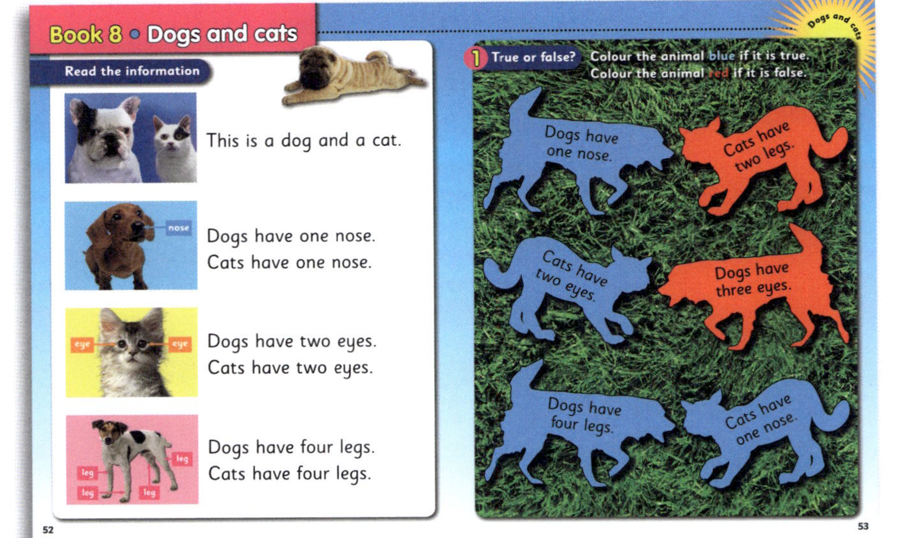

Book 8 • Dogs and cats

Read the information

This is a dog and a cat.

Dogs have one nose.
Cats have one nose.

Dogs have two eyes.
Cats have two eyes.

Dogs have four legs.
Cats have four legs.

52

Dogs and cats

1 True or false? Colour the animal blue if it is true. Colour the animal red if it is false.

53

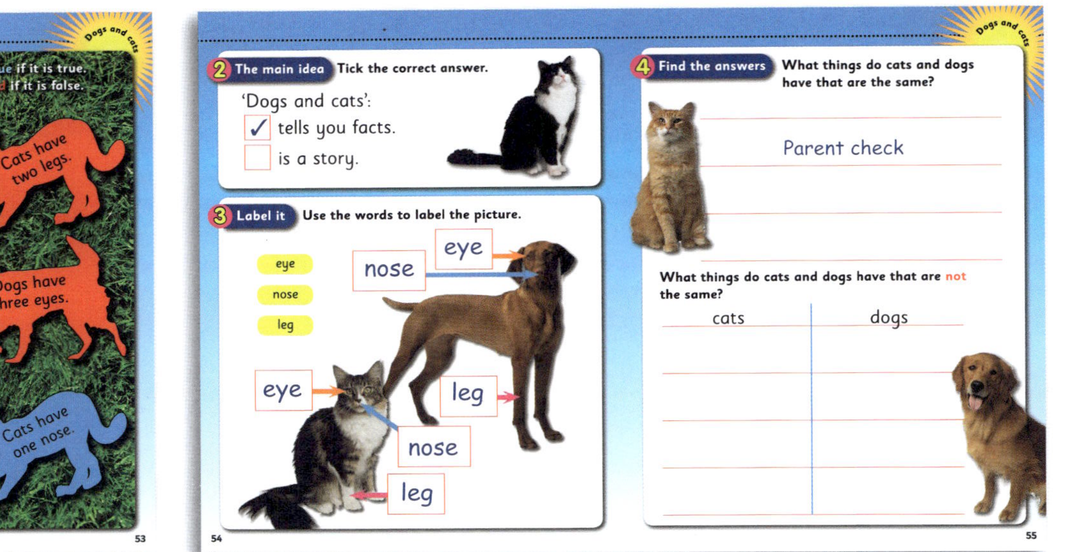

2 The main idea Tick the correct answer.

'Dogs and cats':

- [x] tells you facts.
- [ ] is a story.

3 Label it Use the words to label the picture.

eye
nose
leg

54

Dogs and cats

4 Find the answers What things do cats and dogs have that are the same?

Parent check

What things do cats and dogs have that are not the same?

cats	dogs

55

Answers • Pages 56 to 71

5 Finding out This is a fact book about dogs.

Dogs

Contents page
Chapter 1 Kinds of dogs 1
Chapter 2 What dogs eat 5
Chapter 3 What dogs do 7

Answer these questions.

What is this book about?
Dogs

How many chapters are there?
3

What will page 5 tell you?
What dogs eat

What is chapter 1 called?
Kinds of dogs

56

Dogs and cats

6 Your turn Draw a picture of a cat or dog. Answer the questions about your picture.

Parent check

What is it called?

What does it eat?

What does it do?

57

Book 9 • My five senses

Read the information

We have five senses.
I can see with my eyes.
I can see a butterfly.

I can hear with my ears.
I can hear music.

I can smell with my nose.
I can smell a flower.

I can taste with my tongue.
I can taste an apple.

I can touch with my hands.
I can touch the sand.

58

My five senses

1 Yes or no? Colour yes or no.

We have three senses. yes **no**

I can hear with my ears. **yes** no

I can touch things with my hands. **yes** no

My tongue helps me to see. yes **no**

59

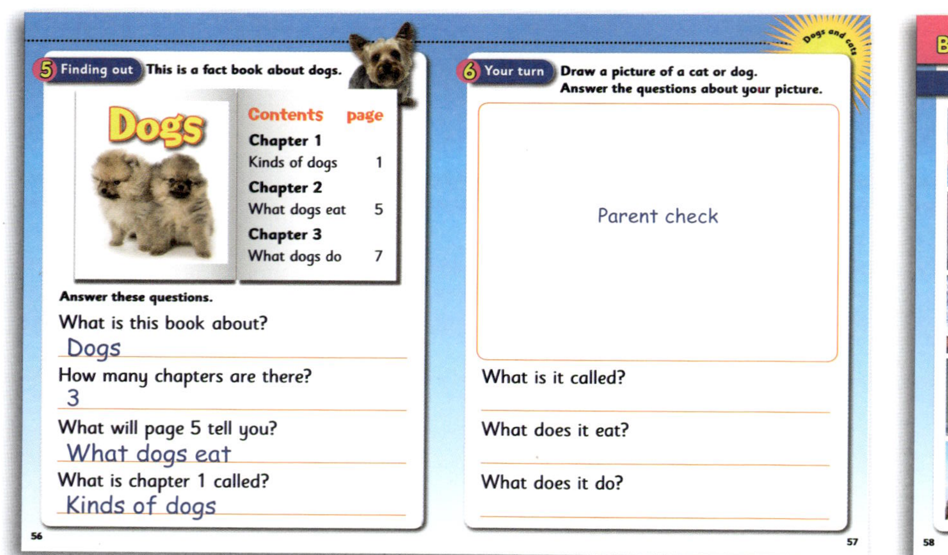

My five senses

2 The main idea Tick the correct answer.

'My five senses' is:
☐ a story.
✓ about real life.

3 Match up Complete the list of senses. Match them to the correct body part.

see
t ouch
t aste
h ear
s mell

60

My five senses

4 Find the answers What things can humans and cats do that are the same?

Parent check

What things can humans and cats do that are not the same?

humans	cats

61

5 Your turn Write three things that you can ...

Parent check

see

smell

taste

touch

hear

62

My five senses

6 What happened? Number the events in order from 1 – 4. Write what happens next.

Chop the apple. 3

Get an apple. 1

Put the apple on a plate. 4

Peel the apple. 2

Then

63

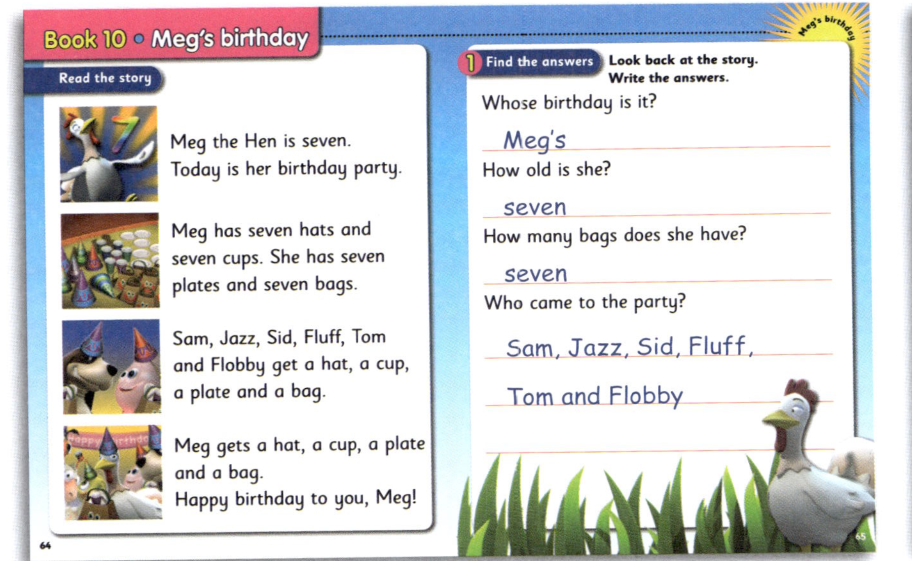

Book 10 • Meg's birthday

Read the story

Meg the Hen is seven.
Today is her birthday party.

Meg has seven hats and seven cups. She has seven plates and seven bags.

Sam, Jazz, Sid, Fluff, Tom and Flobby get a hat, a cup, a plate and a bag.

Meg gets a hat, a cup, a plate and a bag.
Happy birthday to you, Meg!

64

1 Find the answers Look back at the story. Write the answers.

Whose birthday is it?
Meg's

How old is she?
seven

How many bags does she have?
seven

Who came to the party?
Sam, Jazz, Sid, Fluff,
Tom and Flobby

65

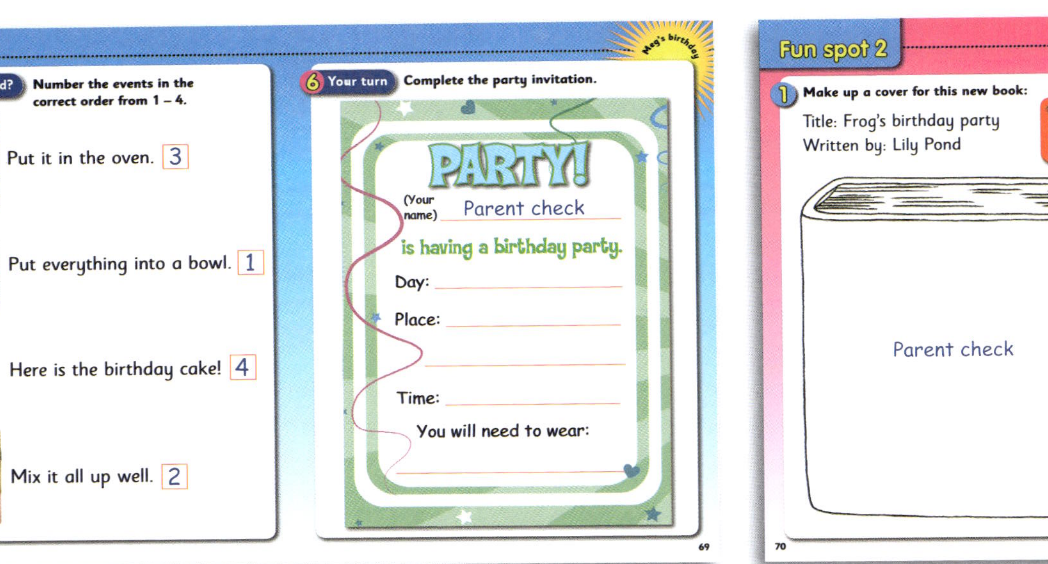

2 The main idea Tick the correct answer.

This story is about:

- [ ] Flobby's birthday party.
- [ ] Meg's birthday presents.
- [x] Meg's 7th birthday party.

3 Match up Match each word to the correct picture.

hats, shells, cups, tail, cake, sea, plates, fish

66

4 Step-by-step Follow each step to decorate the cake.

- Write **Meg** on the cake.
- Draw seven candles on the cake.
- Draw seven spotty eggs on the cake.
- Colour the bow purple.
- Colour the cake pink.

67

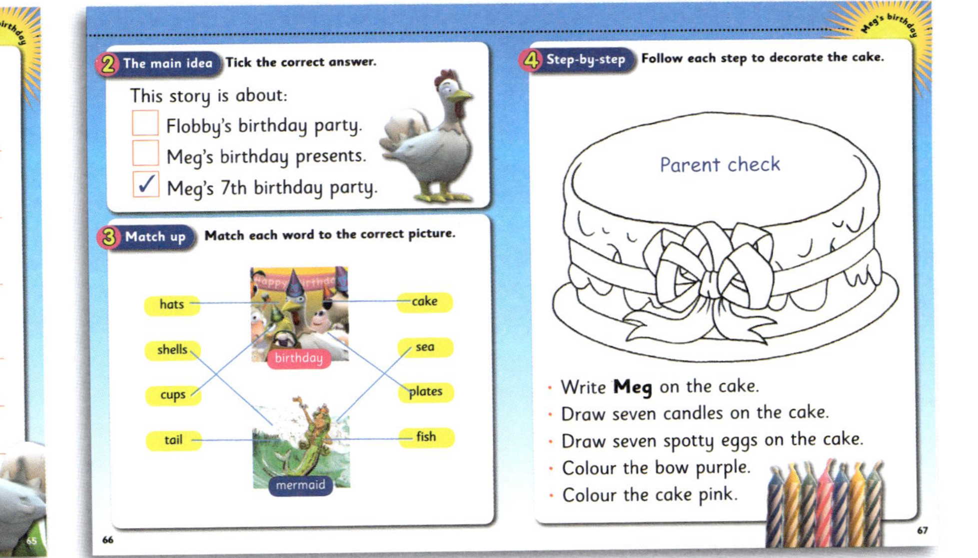

5 What happened? Number the events in the correct order from 1 – 4.

Put it in the oven. 3

Put everything into a bowl. 1

Here is the birthday cake! 4

Mix it all up well. 2

68

6 Your turn Complete the party invitation.

69

Fun spot 2

1 Make up a cover for this new book:

Title: Frog's birthday party
Written by: Lily Pond

Remember
You will also need to draw a picture on the front cover.

70

2 Read how to find the buried treasure. Draw the way on the map.

- Start at the ship. Swim to the rocks.
- Walk to the tree.
- Walk to the hill.
- Climb up to the top of the hill.
- Walk down the hill.
- Walk to the cave. Dig here for treasure!

71

ABC
Reading
eggs
WOW!
You're
amazing!